Table of Contents

WHAT HAS THIS BOOK IN STORE FOR YOU

Since the beginning of times, nature has been a source of inspiration to connoisseurs of art, painters, wanderers, and writers. Many photographers stepping into the world of visual arts consider it mandatory to master landscape photography. Depicting the wonders and secrets of the nature accurately through photography may seem like an easy task but as a matter of fact, there are too many intricacies involved. However, the art of landscape photography is not esoteric, and with practice, precaution, and precision, you will be able to take breathtaking award-winning pictures of mesmerizing landscapes.

Capturing masterpiece landscape shots is a challenging task. Grasping the elements of what constitutes a great picturesque shot will help you in your quest to become a better landscape photographer. This book covers all the fundamentals of landscape photography. It doesn't matter whether you are reading the book to quench your curiosity about the secrets of taking the perfect picture of the scenic views or want to enhance your photography skills — the eBook aims at taking your ambitions and knowledge about landscape photography to the next-level.

You will learn the following aspects of the landscape photography in this eBook:

+ What landscape photography is all about;
+ The perfect gear and lens for taking the best landscape shots;
+ The various important camera setting for capturing the scenery;
+ The importance of depth field in landscape photography and how to achieve it;
+ Tips for taking interesting landscape images;
+ The mysterious art of taking the award-winning landscape shots — the golden time to shoot images; and
+ The different styles of landscape photography

It is hoped that through this eBook, your learning curve about landscape photography rises, and you are able to utilize the techniques described throughout the content well. You will marvel at the different perspectives there are to view the same object and the best way to seize the moment. As you reach the ending, you can be certain of the fact that, you will not only be enthralled but would have fallen in love with the beauties of nature all over again — this time your passion for landscape photography will be more profound and endless. With this eBook, you are bound to go on an expedition of your own. So stay hooked!

WHAT IS LANDSCAPE PHOTOGRAPHY ALL ABOUT

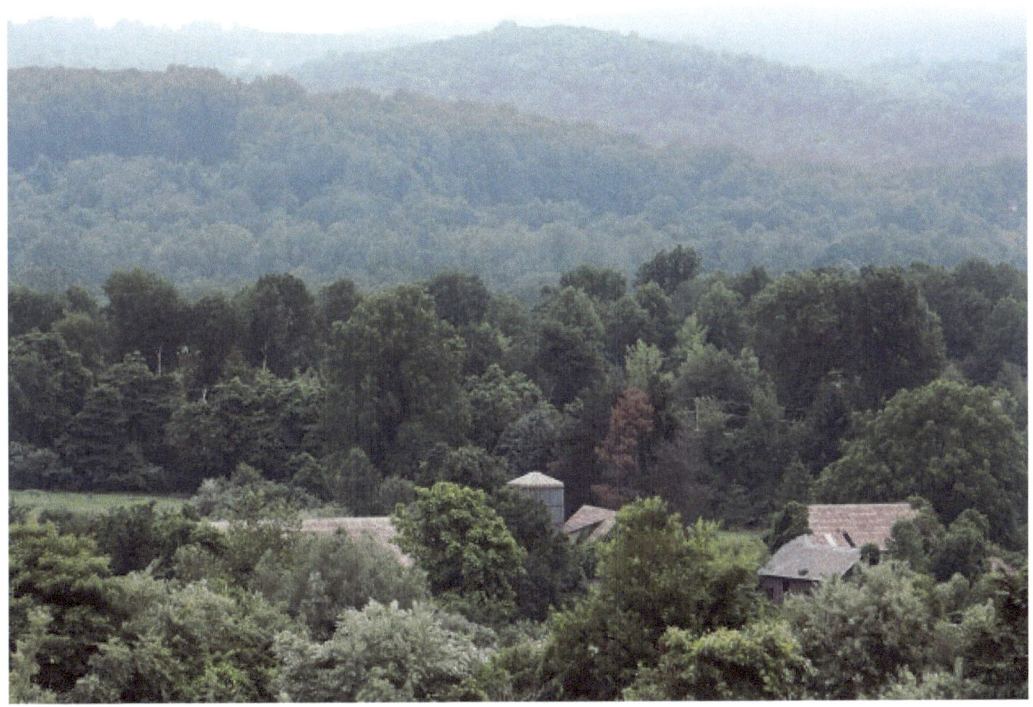

Being a landscape photographer is an interesting job or a hobby. It often drags one into answering questions like "What is landscape photography all about?" It wouldn't be wrong to state that landscape photography is about depicting macroscopic and microscopic elements of nature — the crimson sky at the dusk, a lone tree at the top of the highest peak of a mountain, gushing rivers, or the rising sun at the crack of dawn. The bookish definition would be that landscape photography is about taking pictures of the landscape or the nature.

But that's not all — landscape photography is so much more than the mere art of taking pictures of the landscapes, representing the sceneries. Landscape photography is purposeful. A great picture of a landscape lets the viewer connect with it. It tells the observers a story. There is conviction in the statement that a picture is worth a thousand words, and skillful landscape photographer accomplishes exactly that — capturing the instants of time — transforming even the most simplistic objects into something quite extraordinary.

A landscape photographer does not always show the people the world in its glorified state. In fact, the beauty and uniqueness is found even in the commonplace objects. So in order for a landscape picture to stand out, it does not have to be taken in an awe-inspiring backdrop. After all beauty lies in the eyes of the beholder, and a great landscape photograph allows the viewers to look beyond the objects depicted in the picture. You press the shutter of the camera, and *cepit momento.* You have taken a shot that allows the human being to reconnect with the fundamental elements of nature.

The main aspect of landscape photography is to show the world in its most frail form as well as the most exultant form, making the observers more aware of their surroundings. A great landscape image intensifies feelings and emotions. It allows the viewers to examine the beauty of nature, and know that it is volatile. It needs to be protected, marveled at, and appreciated.

What Makes Landscape Photography Challenging?

The main reason why landscape photography is so challenging is that your boundaries are constrained within the confinements of the land. The visual art of landscape photography is made more complex because of the fact that you cannot use the elements of cinematography in it — no sound effects and music to enhance the beauty. All that you have is the natural world spread before your eyes, and your gadgets. Of course, you may add effects later on but you do not get to benefit from the studio lighting for detailing while taking the images. In most cases when taking a landscape image, the setting is static but the image has to be dynamic, and to top it all, you have the burden of adding as much depth as you can within the two dimensional end product.

Now that we have described what landscape photography is all about, conveyed the idea that it is a challenging task, and established the criterion for a great landscape picture, it is time to begin learning about the elements of landscape photography.

BEST LENS AND GEAR FOR LANDSCAPE PHOTOGRAPHY

A landscape photographer connects with the soul of the beholder — bringing them closer to nature. Being a landscape photographer often takes you on expeditions, which requires you to carry your camera with you everywhere you travel. In order to take a magnificent picture, you must acknowledge the importance of the gear and the camera systems. This is because if you do not have the right camera system, you will be constrained to take certain landscape pictures. Whether it is a star trail photograph that requires an intervalometer or a macrograph that requires a macro lens, the right gear is of utmost significance.

This section will examine appropriate lens and gear necessary to take inspirational landscape photographs.

Camera

The technological advancements have revolutionized cameras to a great extent. With any random off-the-shelf DSLR camera, you can capture stunning landscape photographs. An important thing to remember is that the photo equipment ought to be extremely reliable and should be able to handle the temperature extremes. Why is that the case? Well, the best landscape photographs are often taken in daunting weather conditions — for instance, an image taken at the dawn in below freezing point temperature, or in a stormy weather with strong winds blowing. Imagine the sand blowing in your eyes in an African desert while the scorching sun fries your skin — and you have to capture the perfect shot in that condition.

Nikon D700 and D750 are sturdy and have a high performance. Fuji Film X-T10 is one of the best auto-focusing cameras in the market. Fuji Film X-T1 has an impenetrable seal, which makes it perfect for capturing images in the wet climatic zones.

How to Choose the Camera System?

In landscape photography, the sharpness of the image is the real essence, which is attained with an aperture that provides an exceptional field depth. Idyllically, the aperture range must be between f/9 and f/16.

Here are some of the factors that you should keep in mind when setting out to buy the camera systems:

- Is the camera system protected with weather sealing?
- Is there a shutter speed setting (bulb mode) available that elongates the exposure duration?
- What is the exposure time — is it long?
- Can you change the ISO setting — that is, can you change the sensitivity to light?
- Can you control the shutter speed and aperture manually?

Film Camera Systems or Digital Camera Systems — Which Camera Selection Is Ideal?

The debate about making a selection between film camera systems and the digital camera systems for landscape photography is an endless one. Well, both have their perks and the downsides. You might wonder why there are landscape photographers who are still interested in the analog film format. There are many professional landscape photographers use film camera systems with both large and medium formats — the latter has the tendency to capture high-resolution images. An astounding 400 MP image can be obtained from medium format films. Obviously, if you compare the resolution of an ordinary 35mm film camera with the high-tech digital camera, the image quality of the latter will definitely be better. Apart from the resolution, digital camera systems are winning the race in all other aspects, such as, the sensitivity to light and dynamic range.. The quality of the sensor of the digital camera also helps in determining the noise in the resultant image.

Lens

Unarguably, the lens is the most significant equipment for a landscape photographer. It does not matter how good the camera system is, if the mounted lens is not of superlative quality, the image will not turn out well. In landscape photography, the lenses vary to a great extent..

Here are some of the lenses that you should be concerned with respect to the landscape photography.

1. Ultra Wide Angle Lens

Simply put, landscape photography cannot be done without the ultra wide angle (UWA) lens. So if there is just one lens that you can isolate for landscape photography, UWA is the one. But what makes this lens so idyllic for shooting landscapes? Actually, these lenses offer a greater field view along with the necessary depth of field. There are two types of UWA lenses:

- Prime
- Zoom

The prime UWA lenses are mostly cheaper and produce high quality image. They allow the photographer to shoot at wide apertures, for instance f/2.8. This is particularly helpful when you are capturing the stars. However, a major disadvantage of the prime lens is that the focal length is restrictive and you will have to change your position if you want to "zoom" the image.

On the contrary, the zoom lens gives you the liberty of adjusting to a variety of different focal lengths. Seascapes are best captured with zoom lenses. The main reason is that you might not be able to adjust the lens with the help of feet movement.

The field view of the UWA prevents you from combining panoramic images. The horizon, with the help of UWA, appears further than it usually is, which makes the landscape photograph appear wider.

2. Macro Lens

The macro lenses are able to magnify the objects up to 10 times the actual size of the image. This lens is beneficial if you want to capture the diminutive beauties of nature. Other lenses in the kit may not be able to enhance the details. However, while you can take quality images with a macro lens, you will have to use a tripod. This is because when you are taking an image with a macro lens, the camera-shaking tendency also gets magnified with the object magnification. The shallow depth of the lens forces you to decide which parts of the object you would like to focus more.

Here are some of the best camera lenses that are available for macrographs:

- 65mm Canon MPE
- 90mm Tamron f/2.8
- 105mm Nikkor f/2.8
- 100mm Canon f/2.8

Extension tubes placed between the camera and the lens are also a great way to achieve the desired results. These allow the lens to extend closer to the object. Macro flash allows you to capture the image that cannot be taken in natural light, thereby, increasing the field depth.

3. Telephoto lens

This type of lens is best for wildlife photography. So, if you do not want to distract the animals while capturing landscape image, the telephoto lens is the best lens for the purpose. It is a powerful long lens that enlarges the objects present at distance. These make the objects seem bigger while also giving the image a shallow depth, making the focus strong, and isolating the object of interest. There are 70 mm telephoto lenses available, which can take superb landscape images. However, the range often extends to 400 mm lenses. In the landscape photography, the compositions achieved with the telephoto lens are quite unique as compared to that of the regular ultra wide lens. As opposed to the ultra wide lens, the telephoto lens compresses the depth of the field. The telephoto lens will add a multitude of layers to the landscape photograph. You can use it to your benefit and add the desired depth to the picture — i.e. you make the objects appear closer to one another. The higher the quality of the lens, the more it will cost.

4. Midrange lens

Midrange zoom lenses can also help you take mind-blowing landscape photographs. The midrange zoom lens has the ability to capture the shots at relatively wide angle because of the zoom. The range typically lies in between 18mm at the wide end and 70 mm at the long end. There are several versatile midrange zooms in the market that allow you to capture images at wide focal lengths as well, providing a longer reach simultaneously. These lenses prove to be quite a tool for the traveling photographers. On a downside, the midrange lenses are generally slower as they are typically, f/5.6 at the longer end and f 3.5 at the wider end.

Essential Filters for Landscape Photography

Filters can prove to be of great help to a landscape photographer. Any professional photographer will agree that they are necessary for enhancing landscape photography. Sometimes, it is impossible to capture a great shot without filters as they assist in getting the accurate exposure.

But, there are so many different filters that one may get confused which one should be used for landscape photography. Here are three of the classiest filters that you will ever need to improve your landscape images:

1. Neutral Density Filters

Capturing eye-catching images at wide angles is one of the challenges that landscape photographers often face. The hurdle can be removed by using neutral density filters. So, if you are planning to go on an adventurous trip to shoot snow-capped mountains, do not forget to carry the neutral density filter along. But, what is the benefit of using this filter? Well, in order to understand the advantage of this filter, you need to grasp the problem first. When you are taking images of flowing water like waterfall or rain, you want the result to be smooth and foggy, which means that the shutter speed ought to be really low and the camera must be mounted on a tripod. Now, if you are shooting the image in day time when the sun is shining bright, it is not possible to accomplish the desired result even if you decrease ISO and increase the f-number. This is where the neutral density filter comes into action — they minimize the amount of light entering the lens. Consequently, the shutter speed is reduced and the exposure time is increased. You cannot achieve the same result without using the neutral density filter at the time of post-processing. The neutral density filters have a large range of the aperture-lens control and they can blur the movement of objects in motion to a greater extent as compared to the polarizing filter.

2. Polarizing Filters

These filters are the ultimate tool for landscape photography. So, if there is just one filter that you can restrict yourself to, this must be it. The polarizing filter enhances saturation, which makes the colors richer and vibrant. If you are shooting green foliage, grasslands or the blue skies, polarizing filters will be of great assistance. Also, these are best for minimizing reflections — therefore, these can eliminate the reflective glare and sheen from rocks, trees, water, and other glistening objects. Basically, you will be able to see the rocks clearly under the flowing waters when you use this filter. The sky could be darkened so that the clouds can be captured vividly. As a novice, you may get a circular polarizer to fit in front of the camera lens, and then simply rotate it to get the desired levels of polarization. The circular polarizer is easy to handle. Additionally, you may also procure a polarizing filter that has the following coatings:

+ Skylight coating
+ Warm tone coating
+ Intensifying and enhancement coatings
+ UV Haze 2a coating

Thee coatings will saturate colors more than a typical; polarizing filter. If you are making use of a warm tone polarizing filter, make sure that the white balance settings are appropriate — never use auto settings, either use custom settings or set it to "sunny". An important strategy to implement when you are using polarizing filter is to adjust the frame with caution for most effectiveness. The polarizer yields best results when the sun is shining from the side rather than glistening directly on the top or from the behind.

It is also necessary to know that polarizer do not work well when you are shooting images at extremely wide angled lens, which means lens that are wider than:

+ 24 mm on cameras with full frame;
+ 35 mm on cameras with medium format; and
+ 16 mm on cameras with APS-C format

The aforementioned lenses will cause the sky to darken unevenly and cause a vignette at the edges of the landscape photograph.

3. Graduated Neutral Density Filter

Ordinary neutral density filter only limits the light entering the lens of the camera. These filters reduce the amount of light evenly across the entire space. However, if you want to attain a gradient effect in the landscape image, then you will have to use a graduated neutral density filter. For example, you want to have an effect that reduces the shadowy effects from the bottom of the image but darkens the top portion of the photograph, you will need to have a graduated density filter as it would subject the top portion of the lens to less light as compared to the bottom area. These filters are extremely beneficial for capturing landscape images when the sky is much brighter than the background. The filter will allow you to adjust the light exposure accurately while retaining the shadows and highlights of the original scenery. The strengths of graduated neutral density filters are of varying numbers. The most commonly used ones are 0.9, 0.6, and 0.3. These strengths correspond to 3, 2, and 1 f-stop minimization of light in the darkest of areas.

It is essential to know that since the composition plays an important role in determining the size of the sky versus the background, these filters come in rectangular shape. This means that these filters can be used optimally when they are coupled with a holder system. Choosing the filter holder system is also quite daunting as a wrong one can cause vignetting. The graduated density filters are also available in various tints.

4. Warming Filters

The real problem with outdoor photography is that the lighting may not favor you. Mesmerizing shots rely heavily upon good lighting. So, if you have an overcast sky, your photographs will look dull, and they will contain a bluish pall. While digital cameras can auto adjust this problem with white balance, most film cameras require additional warming filters. Your landscape photographs taken at dusk and dawn do not have to be uninspiring anymore, as the warming filter will give the shots an orange tinge. This would reduce the bluish tones and make your images more animated. However, with the development of Photoshop software, the warming effect can also be attained after the picture has been captured at the time of editing. Therefore, this filter isn't as important as it used to be in the past.

CAMERA SETTINGS

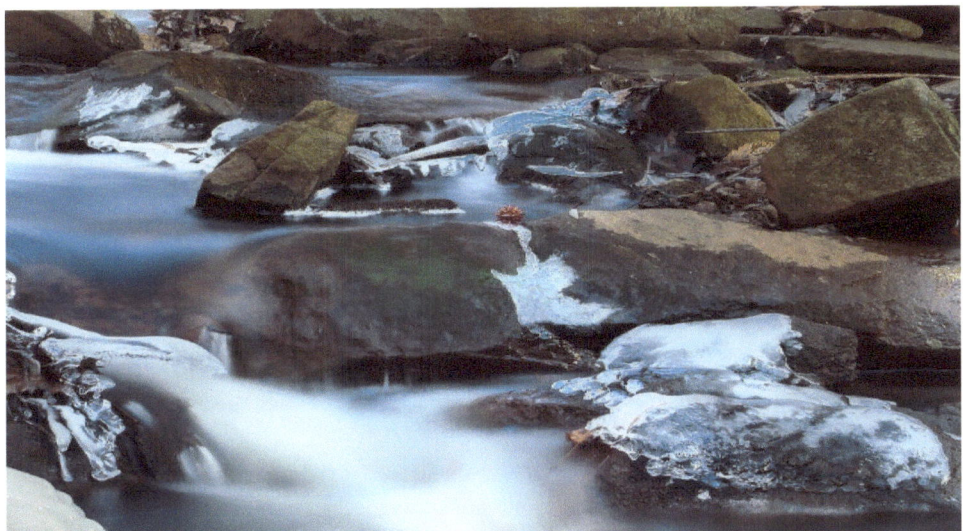

When the landscape photography is done accurately, it produces stunning results. Amateurs might wonder why their images do not look as enthralling as the ones taken by professional photographers. Apart from post-processing and impeccable composition, it is really the camera settings that make a huge difference on the landscape photographs. Therefore, it is essential that before you think about pressing the shutter, you have used appropriate settings. Before delving into the settings, it ought to be highlighted that all or most of the following settings are controlled automatically in case there isn't a manual setting feature on your camera.

Most Important Camera Settings

Essentially, there are three main camera settings that you must get right whenever you are taking a landscape photo:

- ISO Setting;
- Shutter Speed; and
- Aperture

These settings are also known as the pillars of photography; their importance can never be over-emphasized. All of these camera settings control the amount of light entering the lens. We shall explore the impact of these settings and their purpose in this topic.

1. Aperture

Aperture is a hole contained within the camera lens. It is the aperture through which the light passes and reaches the main body of the camera. As the camera is analogous to the human eye, the equivalents of the cornea will be the lens. All the external light falls on the front portion of the lens and then travels to iris. The amount of light determines whether the pupil will shrink or expand. The pupil is a hole that allows the light to pass deeper. In photography, the pupil and the aperture are analogous to each other. The camera sensor behaves like the retina of the eye and the amount of light that falls on it is determined by the size of the pupil, equivalently, the size of the aperture. The iris, in the field of optics, is also known as the diaphragm, which is responsible for controlling the size of the aperture.

The aperture is articulated in f-numbers. The f-numbers are also termed as f-stops. The aperture setting is defined as the ratio of the focal length and the size of the camera hole (aperture). The f-stop lets one know the actual size of the aperture — how open or close it really is. A smaller f-stop indicates that the aperture is large in size. Conversely, a larger f-number means that the aperture is small. To most beginners, this concept may appear confusing. For instance, f/1.4 is much bigger than f/5.6. The

How Does the Aperture Impact the Depth of Field?

The aperture settings affect the depth of field greatly, which is the level of sharpness behind and in front of the target object. The following summary will make things simpler for you to understand:

- *Lower f number —wide aperture —lesser the depth of field —hazier background*
- *Higher f number —narrow aperture —greater the depth of field —sharper foreground*

This means that a lower f-number will correspond with a shallow field depth whilst a higher f-number will correspond to a greater depth of field. The depth of field keeps the attention of the observer on the main target. Albeit the target is distant in the landscape photography, controlling the depth of field is still extremely important. The background in the landscape photography is also interesting as the main subject.

2. Shutter Speed

The shutter of a camera determines the point in time after the light strikes the lens when the sensor will close or open. Specifically, the shutter speed points out towards the light exposure — the faster the speed of the shutter, the lesser the exposure time. Most cameras available today are able to control the shutter speeds between $\frac{1}{4000} X \, 1 \, second \, and \, \frac{1}{800} X \, 1 \, second$ as the shortest speeds while the longest speeds are in the range of 15 seconds or 30 seconds.

The shutter speed is also used to cease the motion of the image and the camera alike (especially, if the landscape image is not being shot with the help of a tripod). Even the slightest bit of camera motion will make the image hazy. In order to prevent motion from making the image blurry when capturing the image with your hands, you will have to set the shutter speed as $\frac{1}{x}$. Here, x is twice the focal length at which you are taking the shot. For example at 100 mm you must set the shutter speed as $\frac{1}{200} X\ 1\ sec$.

You can avoid making the image blurry by delaying the exposure. This setting prevents the exposure from starting prior to the desired time. This is particularly beneficial to avoid camera vibration when the finger presses the shutter. Yes, some vibration occurs even when you are using a tripod. Therefore, the timer mode helps you in this regard a great deal.

Is motion a bad phenomenon for a landscape photographer? Well, not at all! In fact polished photographer absolutely love to capture the photographs in motion — waterfalls, rainfalls, rivers, brooks, and streams. In such circumstances, however, it is ideally preferred that a tripod is used. Just be absolutely certain that the shutter speed you are using is only fast enough for you to grab hold of the camera steadily so that you can prevent the camera from shaking. If you are dropping the shutter speed below $\frac{1}{30} X\ 1\ sec$, then you will have to take the photograph with the help of a tripod. Just in case a tripod is not available you can still capture a perfect landscape image by using ISO setting between 200 and 400. ISO setting will be explained in depth later in this section. Experiment with various shutter speed settings at varying differences when you are shooting outdoor image so that you get an idea about the accurate speed. Ideally, flowing water can best be captured at a shutter speed of $\frac{1}{500} X\ 1\ sec$ at

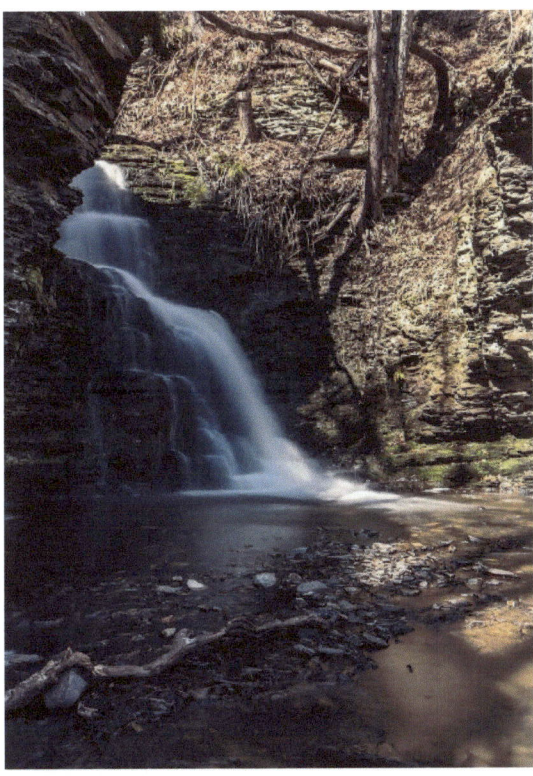

a distance. However, if you are taking a close-up of a flying bird or flowing water, then it is preferable to use a shutter speed of $\frac{1}{2000} X\ 1\ sec$. These shutter speed are not exact and you can experiment with your own preferred settings.

How Does the Aperture Impact the Shutter Speed?

The f-number also affects the speed of the shutter. When you are using a lower f-number, it implies that the amount of light entering the lens is greater. This means that there is no need for the shutter to stay open for a longer exposure time, which further indicates that you keep a faster shutter image to take a fantastic landscape shot. Conversely, a higher f-number means that the amount of light entering is less so you need to increase the exposure time, which means that there is a need for a slower shutter speed.

3. ISO Setting

ISO setting in digital cameras is actually the same as the film speed in traditional cameras. In digital cameras, it is basically responsible for controlling the sensitivity of the camera with respect to the light. The range of the ISO settings is vast and ideally, varies from 100 to 6400 and sometimes even higher. Just like the shutter speed, the ISO speed also correlates with the increment and the decrement of the exposure. But, contrary to the shutter speed and the aperture setting, a higher ISO setting will add noise to the image. Therefore, a lower ISO setting is generally preferable. This means that the ISO setting is always kept at its least value until and unless it is impossible to attain the desired aperture or the shutter speed settings. Commonly used ISO settings are: 800, 400, 200, and 100. In high quality digital cameras, you can use a range of ISO setting between 50 and 800.

ACHIEVING THE DEPTH OF FIELD IN LANDSCAPE PHOTOGRAPHY

In photography, depth of field is an important concept, especially if you want to master landscape photography. Depth of field is generally described as the zone within a photograph that has an acceptable level of sharpness, which will be in the focus. This zone differs from one image to another, and may lie either in front of the image or in the foreground. As mentioned earlier, the aperture size has a direct and significant impact on the depth of field. Let's now understand how to get a sharply focused landscape photograph.

In order to attain a greater depth of field, it is important that the focal length is short and the aperture is narrow, which means that the f-stops are large — that is, between f/8 and f/22. To a landscape photographer, it is essential to know how to maximize the depth of field.

How to Get the Maximum Depth of Field?

Make use of a tripod to shoot the landscape photographs, which does not just play a major role in getting long exposures but it also allows you to focus the target better. Here is what you need to do to get mesmerizing well-focused images:

- Keep the camera on manual mode and set the focal so that it fits the screen perfectly — the wider the angle, the greater will be the depth of field.
- Calculate the hyperfocal distance with help of an online calculator or an app installed on your phones. Enter a value that is little greater than the calculated hyperfocal distance.
- These settings will allow all the target objects, from half of the hyperfocal length to the horizon, to be in sharp focus.
- You can make use of the auto focus to focus at any desired point located at the hyperfocal distance. Revert to the manual setting and lock the value of the focus.
- If you are taking the shot with a DSLR, then make use of mirror lock up to avoid the mechanical shocks from disrupting the image.
- In landscape photography, the key is to focus the objects that are at a distance.

- Ideally, to produce more depth of field, keep the focal length at 10 mm – 35 mm.

The reason why a larger depth of field is desired in landscape photography is that it ensures that the objects in the foreground, middle, and those in the distance are sharply focused. So, if you always get the mountains at the distance blurred when shooting landscape photographs, it is focusing at the hyperfocal distance that does the trick, and accomplishes the maximum depth of field.

Factors That Affect the Depth of Field
The depth of field is dependent upon the following factors:

- Aperture
- Focal length
- Circle of Confusion
- Focus Distance

Circle of confusion is the tiniest element of an image that holds on to the "identifiable" details. The hyperfocal distance is that distance at which the lens is focused and everything henceforth from the half hyperfocal distance till the horizon (infinity) will be in acceptable focus range — this is based upon the circle of confusion, aperture, and focal length. It is extremely difficult to focus at the hyperfocal distance. Just make sure that when you are focusing, the distance is approximately 2 -3 feet longer as compared to the hyperfocal distance for sharper focus. However, if you keep the focus less than the hyperfocal distance, then the target object will not be in proper focus.

THE IMPORTANCE OF COMPOSITION IN LANDSCAPE PHOTOGRAPHY

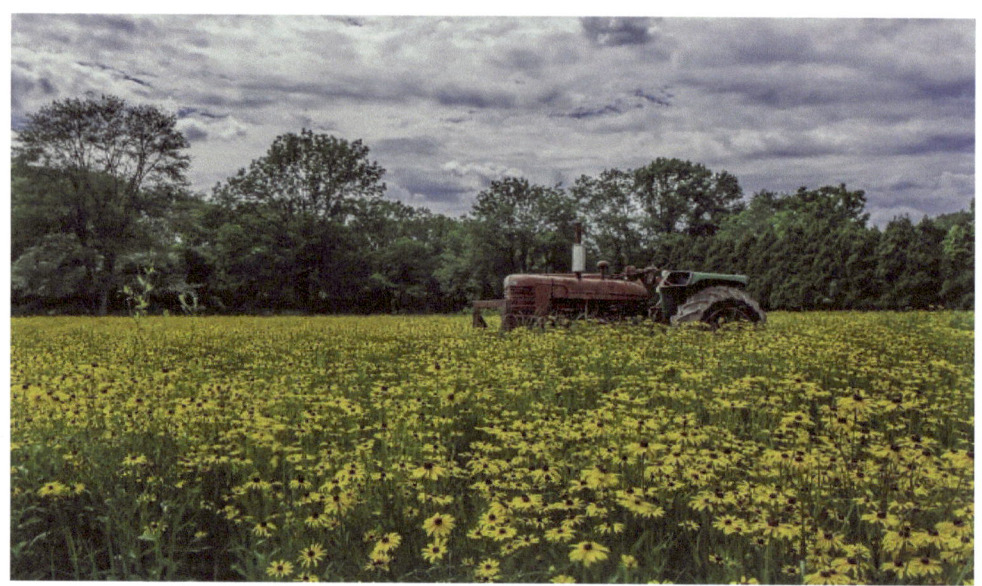

Composition is the primary element of all types of photography. It is the composition that breathes life into the static images. There aren't any predefined or impregnable rules of composition. However, the following guidelines play a vital role in differentiating between a vivid and animated landscape photograph, and a boring or lifeless image. The four guidelines of composition for taking breathtaking landscapes are as follows:

1. Rule of Thirds

Scout the area that you are interested in capturing really well. Discover the ideal spot from which you can take your shots. Make use of your photographer's instinct and analyze the time when the light is just perfect for the images. Then, when you are composing, visually divide the image into portions — draw four imaginary lines: two horizontal and two vertical. Now, you may keep the target right in the center. However, in most situations, it is better to place your target away from the center. Keep moving away until the target moves away from the center and intersects any one of the imaginary lines. Following this technique will make your landscape photographs interesting and the layout will be appealing to the observers.

2. Diagonal Lines

Whenever you are composing a landscape image, the creative usage of the diagonal lines will make the image more dynamic as opposed to capturing images with horizontal or vertical lines. The diagonal lines are effective in drawing the gaze of the observer straight to the main primary focus. By diagonal lines, it is meant that the path followed by the trees, brooks, or fences is represented diagonally rather than being straight. If you are able to "converge" two diagonal paths at a single point in the landscape photograph, you will succeed in seizing the attention of the viewers.

3. Geometric Shapes

Did you know that even in nature, the geometric patterns have a substantial importance? When you are shooting landscape images, try to position the main elements or the primary targets upon the points of geometric shapes. This is the best way to achieve coherence and balance in the photograph. Your landscape will be outstanding and abstract at the same time. Use the power of your discernment as a photographer and see the landscape in terms of lines and geometrical patterns and use them effectively while composing the scene.

4. Framing the Landscapes

It is important to capture interesting elements in the foreground of the image. However, adding exciting and interesting objects at the edges of the landscape photograph will add a spark to the end result. This technique is referred to as "framing the shot". Overhanging branches, tall trees, and even a bridge may be perfect for framing. When you are composing, ascertain that your frame is aligned accurately. You may also make use of vertical and horizontal lines to align your camera.

THE GOLDEN TIME TO SHOOT LANDSCAPE IMAGES

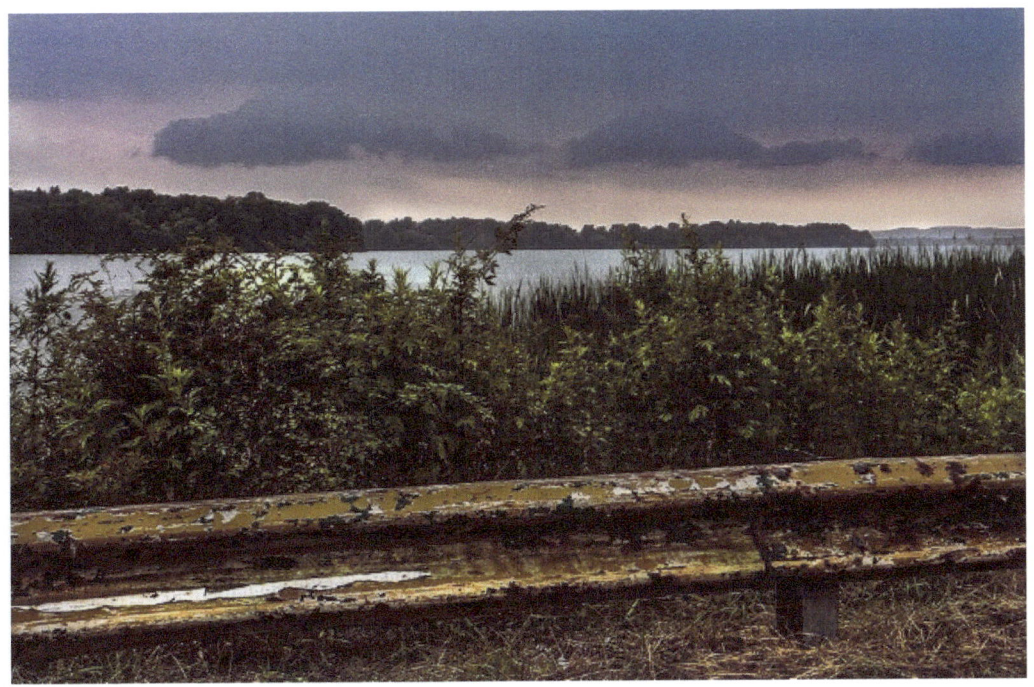

You must have definitely come across the term "golden photography hours" at least once in your lifetime even if you are not a professional photographer. What exactly is meant by the golden time or the golden photography hours? As photographers, the core task is to capture the light at an opportune time — the time when the sunlight at the horizon is low. It is the ideal moment to capture your images. The following periods of time are typically referred to as the golden hours:

- The hour before the sunset
- The hour immediately after the sunrise

Why Is the Image Shot at Midday Dull and Uninspiring?

The natural sunlight can be characterized as soft and harsh. The latter is the one that you experience when the sun is at the zenith on a cloudless day. This is the time when the light is intense and it shines upon the objects from above directly. When you are shooting landscapes in such a light, the warmth is reduced and the contrast is high as explained earlier. The unwelcoming effects in the sky make it necessary for you to take pictures with the help of filters, which may not always be available. In harsh light, the targets are well-lit, undoubtedly — however, they are only lit from a particular direction only. This is why the images that are shot during noon are boring and uninspiring. Capturing even the most spectacular objects in such a light will be one of the most challenging things to do.

What Happens When the Sun Sets or When It Is Rising?

Reduction In the Amount of Contrast

As soon as the sun starts to set in the horizon, and the sunset is approaching this entire scenario changes considerably. What are the benefits of shooting in the golden hour? Well, at these hours, the high contrast is reduced. For landscape photographs, it is important that the light is soft. The diffused lighting will make the shadows longer and less prominent. The range of the tones will also change significantly, and you will witness that even the clouds in the sky are enlightened differently. In the golden hours, the visual transitions soften subtly.

The Color of the Sky during Golden Hours

The sky during the golden hours sheds a more pronounced impact on the photographs. In the morning, notice that the cooler of the sky depict an aura of coolness — they add a bluish color to the images. In contrast, during the evening just before the sunset, the hues of the sky transforms into red and orange shades, providing the landscape photographs with the desired warmth.

Eye-catching Sun Flare Effects during the Golden Hours

One of the most crucial benefits of the golden hour landscape photography is that you can creatively introduce the sun flare effects in the images. These are ideal to introduce drama and mood into the images. Because the sun is low at the horizon, you can make it one of your targets while aiming for the best landscape shot. When does the flaring occur? Well, typically when the sum is at the edge of your frame or near it, you can witness the flaring effect.

UNDERSTANDING BLUE HOUR LANDSCAPE PHOTOGRAPHY

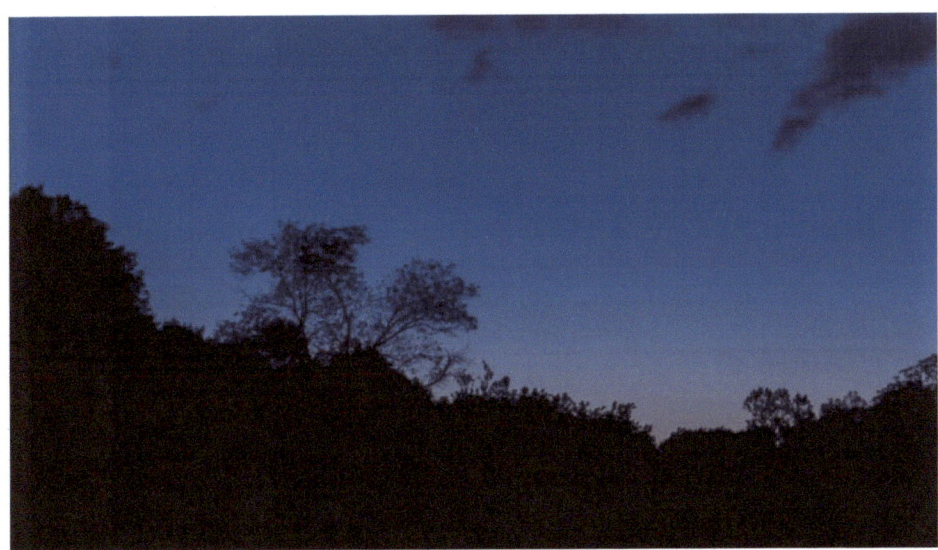

Another important concept to understand when you embark upon the journey of a landscape photographer is the blue hour photography. Apart from daytime and golden hours, blue hour photography also plays an important role in making your landscape images magical. This section will discuss what the blue hour photography really is and why you should capture blue hour landscapes.

What is Blue Hour Photography?

The sky has a deep blue color during the blue hour. The blue hour can be more clearly defined as the time period when the sky changes color from black, to dark blue, and then blue or the other way round. Therefore, the blue hour begins at the as soon as the evening begins, that is, as soon as the golden hour of the sunset ends. Conversely, in the morning, the blue hour begins during the first part of the civil twilight, i.e. just before the sunrise golden hour. The blue hour is an ideal time to capture the moon along with the landscapes. The season and the geographical location will help you determine the length of the blue hour. The time duration during which the sky retains a lustrous deep bluish hue ranges from forty minutes to an hour.

Why Should You Capture Blue Hour Landscapes

The best feature about blue hour photography is that the sky look enthralling and it the ideal time to capture the cloud movements. The blue hour landscapes are dynamic as the shutter speeds are slow and the exposures are longer, which has the tendency to capture the motion perfectly. Most prolific photographers believe that the camera settings are much easier to fix during the blue hour as opposed to the ones set for the daytime images.

Equipment Required For Blue Hour Landscapes

Because of the fact that the exposure time is long for the blue hour photography, a tripod is a must tool for capturing the landscapes. Wide-angle lens would help in framing and composing the blue hour landscapes better. Since darkness will be spreading swiftly, you must carry a flashlight around so that you can scout the land properly. A remote shutter release will also prove to be a handy tool for blue hour landscapes, as it will help in the prevention of camera shaking.

STYLES OF LANDSCAPE PHOTOGRAPHY

Landscapes are portions of a scenic view captured from a single viewpoint. The scenery is the prime subject of the landscape. Therefore, in most landscapes, you will not see humans until and unless, the proportion of these subjects is relatively small within the frame of the landscape. To purists, ideal landscapes are just landscapes — it doesn't depict skylines or the oceans. These are supposed to be cityscapes or seascapes. This is exactly why, there are three characteristic styles of photography, namely:

- Abstract Photography
- Representational Photography
- Impressionistic Photography

1. Abstract Photography

The components of the scenery in abstract photography are depicted graphically. Well, this means that the photographer composes the elements of the landscape in a way that the natural objects are unrecognizable or almost so. The objects are juxtaposed so that the contrast is highlighted and the shapes or the lines are highlighted. Design and geometrical patterns are more essential than a depiction that is recognizable. The photographer focuses on the counter intuitive aspects of the photograph. Typically, an area within the landscape is highlighted.

2. Representational Photography

This is the most realistic form of the landscape photography. It depicts the natural elements of the landscape more clearly and beautifully. The basic approach to this sort of photography is that the captured image is only meant to project the factual components of the image into the minds of the observers. There are no underlying meanings or hidden interpretations that the viewers can draw as opposed to the abstract landscapes. It can simply be termed as a straightforward display of the natural elements of nature. Timing, detailing, and weather conditions are kept in mind when these images are being captured for best results.

3. Impressionistic Photography

This type of photography avails the maximum benefits of the photographic techniques, which makes the image appear vague. This is why these photographs carry an ambience of elusiveness. The impressionist photography make the landscape look unreal. The observer does get to look at the actual scenery but the photographer tries to project an image that isn't true — it is only a representation of the real image.

CONCLUSION

Now that you know about the essential techniques for efficiently capturing the sunlight for breathtaking landscapes, it is time that you start on an adventurous trip of your own. Experiment with the camera settings, and choose the gear wisely. As you step into the world of landscape photography, you will begin to have an entirely new perspective about nature. Every time you position the camera to compose a scenic view, your perspective will make it look outstanding. Only when you have mastered the techniques and learned how use the sunlight for focusing, you can truly lock the grandeur of the scenery into your camera screen.

ABOUT THE AUTHOR

Ryan Crane is a well-known name in international published photography. Ryan developed his photography skills through painstakingly long hours of research and trial and error. Having carved a niche in the world, he now aims to help others who are just stepping into the world of photographic art. Visit ryancranephotography.com to start learning today! Click improveyourphotographyonline.com, if you are a photographer looking to improve their craft.

www.ingramcontent.com/pod-product-compliance
Lightning Source LLC
Chambersburg PA
CBHW040916180526
45159CB00010BA/3093